Raining Cats and Dogs

Jackie White

Copyright © 2015 Jackie White

All rights reserved.

ISBN: **1518676332**
ISBN-13: **978-1518676338**

DEDICATION

For all those wishing to improve their understanding of the French language, and perhaps learn something about their own at the same time. I dedicate this book to my trusty Harrap's French/English dictionary I found in a jumble sale, a faithful friend over 20 years that never fails to deliver the answers to some rather odd questions I keep asking of it.

INTRODUCTION

Language has always fascinated me. Not just the purity of written language, but the word on the street; idiom, sayings, the things we learn from each other that aren't always written down. This language exists in all languages, has a life of its own, ever changing and adapting, no matter your country or culture.

It is also the hardest thing to master if you are learning a new language, as there is no logic sometimes to the things we say. For example, we say, 'Don't count your chickens before they're hatched,' whereas French translates this as, 'Don't sell the skin of the bear before you've killed it."

Suddenly you don't quite know your chickens from your bears, as neither language can adequately explain where these sayings come from (in fact, this would be a great title for a completely separate book.)

Consider this – can you fully understand a direct translation of English phrases in French in a short story written in this manner?

'He looked dipped in soup. "That's the hospital making fun of charity," he said, as I was soaked myself. Choosing the voice of the facility, he didn't argue. We both knew it had all ended up in the fish tail. After all, it was raining twine!'

The real story goes something like this:

'He looked like a drowned rat. "That's the pot calling the kettle black," he said, as I was soaked myself. Choosing the line of least resistance, he didn't argue. We both knew it had all gone haywire. After all, it was raining cats and dogs!'

In one of my previous book, 'Little Black Rammbook', I translated the lyrics of the German band Rammstein. I estimated the number of words our language has, compared with German and French:

> English 1,033,322 words
> German   600,000 words
> French   150,000 words

We have assimilated so many words from other cultures into our own language that there are many different ways of expressing the same thing. For those studying English as a foreign language, these nuances are the hardest thing for them to learn, as their own language probably says it much more directly.

Why did I write this book? It's the follow-on book from its German version with the same title, which is proving so successful it was worth doing for another language.

It's the book I wish I'd had when I was learning French, a reference book to easily look up all the strange things we say and understand how they translate into another language. It will also be a useful reference for French speakers, wanting to improve their English, who can look up English phrases and see how they best translate.

CONTENTS

Introduction ……..   iii

A…………………..   7

B…………………..   9

C…………………. . 16

D………………….   19

E…………………..   23

F…………………..   25

G…………………..   27

H…………………..   32

I…………………..   43

J…………………..   50

K…………………..   51

L…………………..   53

M…………………..   57

N…………………..   58

O…………………..   59

P…………………..   60

Q…………………..   64

R…………………..   65

S…………………..   66

T…………………..   73

U…………………	81
V…………………	82
W…………………	83
X…………………	85
Y…………………	86
Z…………………	88

A

An Englishman's home is his castle

Charbonnier est maître chez soi
A collier is master at his own house
#

All that glitters is not gold

Tout ce qui brille n'est pas or
Everything that shines is not gold
#

A smooth operator

Langue doucereuse
Smooth tongue
#

As plain as the nose on your face

C'est clair comme le jour
That's as clear as the day
#

As sure as eggs are eggs

Aussi sûr que deux et deux font quatre
As sure as two and two make four

A bad egg

Un vaurien
A good-for-nothing/rascal

#

As thick as two short planks

Avoir l'esprit épais
To be dull-witted

#

Another one bites the dust

Il a mordu la poussière
He bit the dust

#

Academically gifted

Bien doué
Well gifted

#

Animal magnetism

Magnétisme animal
Animal magnestism

#

A Little bird told me

Mon petit doigt me l'a dit
My little finger told me

B

Bad blood

La rancune
rancour
#

There is bad blood between them

Il y a de vielles rancunes entre eux
There is old rancour between them
#

Bang your head against a brick wall

Donner de la tête contre un mur
Give your head against a wall
#

Be at loggerheads

Être en conflit avec quelqu'un
Be in conflict with someone
#

Be a pain in the neck

Il me tape sur le système
He taps me on the system

Beggars can't be choosers

Ne choisit pas qui emprunte
Those who borrow haven't a choice
#

Better late than never

Mieux vaut tard que jamais
Better late than never
#

Be in a cold sweat

Être tout en nage
To be all in a swim
#

He's a rough diamond

Ses manières frustes cachent beaucoup de qualités
His rough manners hide many qualities
#

Be in a tight corner

En mauvaise passe
In a bad passing place
#

Be in a tight squeeze (or jam)

On tenait tout juste
One is holding just straight

Be in someone's good books

Être bien vu de quelqu'un
To be well seen by someone
#

Be two-faced

L'hypocrite
The hypocrite
#

Beaver away

Travailler comme quatre
Work like four (people)
#

Between you, me and the gatepost

Soit dit entre nous
Let it be said between us
#

Birds of a feather flock together

Qui se ressemble s'assemble
Those who look like each other assemble together
#

Blood is thicker than water

Nous sommes unis par la voix, la force, du sang
We are united by voice, strength, blood

Blood brother

Compagnon par le cœur
Companion of the heart
#

Be in a deep blue funk

Avoir le cafard
To have the blues
#

Between the Devil and the deep blue sea

Être pris entre deux feux
To be put between two lights
#

Be sold down the river

Trahir, vendre quelqu'un
Betray or sell someone
#

Breathe down someone's neck

Talonner quelqu'un
Hound someone
#

Bottom of the class

Il est le dernier de sa classe
He is last in his class

By the skin of your teeth

S'échapper de justesse
Escaping justice
#

Be in a right mess/sticky wicket

Être dans une situation difficile
Be in a difficult situation
#

Burn the candle at both ends

Brûler la chandelle par les deux bouts
Burn the candle at both ends
#

Bark up the wrong tree

Suivre une fausse piste
Follow a wrong track
#

Be in the pink

Se porter à merveille
Behave as a marvel
#

Blow your top

Sortir de ses gonds
Separate from your hinges

Be on the wrong track

Suivre une mauvaise piste
Follow the wrong path
#

Bird in the hand is worth two in the bush

Un tiens vaut mieux que deux tu l'auras
An interest is worth more than two you might have in the future
#

Be as good as gold

Sage comme une image
As wise as his picture
#

Blind alley

L'impasse
Impasse
#

Be a blockhead

Un lourdaud; gros bête
Oaf; big beast
#

Bursting at the seams

Être plein à éclater
Be ready to explode

Butter wouldn't melt in his mouth

Il fait la sainte nitouche
He's playing Saint Nitouche (little hypocrite)
#

Burn your bridges/boats

Brûler ses vaisseaux
Burn your vessels
#

Beyond belief

Incroyable
Incredible
#

Big bang theory

La théorie du big bang
Theory of the big bang

C

Call a spade a spade

Appeler les choses par leur nom
To call things by their name
#

Cut a long story short

Pour dire la chose en deux mots
Say the thing in two words
#

Chip off the old block

C'est bien le fils de son père
He's certainly his father's son
#

Come down on someone like a ton of bricks

Tomber sur le dos à quelqu'un
Fall on someone's back
#

Carry coals to Newcastle

Porter de l'eau à la rivière
Carry water to the river

Common as muck

Il est assez vulgaire
He is quite vulgar
#

Chop and change (opinion)

Il change d'opinion à tout bout de champ
He changes opinion at every headland
#

Crack open a bottle

Vider une bouteille
Empty a bottle
#

Cool as a cucumber

Avec un sang froid imperturbable
With an unruffled cold blood
#

Don't count your chickens before they've hatched

Il ne faut pas vendre la peau de l'ours avant de l'avoir tué
Don't sell the skin of the bear until you've killed it
#

Come under the influence (of alcohol)

Être sous l'empire de la boisson
To be under the influence of drink

Cock-a-hoop

Fier comme Artaban
As proud as Artaban (the 4th wise man)
#

Charity begins at home

Charité bien ordonnée commence par soi
Charity well-ordered begins with oneself
#

Cut off your nose to spite your face

Bouder contre son ventre
Sulk down into your stomach
#

Cross that bridge when you get to it

Chaque chose en son temps
Everything in its own time

D

Don't beat about the bush

Ne pas y aller par quatre chemins
Don't go there via 4 routes
#

Dead as a Dodo/doorpost

Mort et enterré
Dead and buried
#

Don't worry yourself (your little head) about it

Ne vous inquiétez pas !
Don't worry yourself!
#

Don't count your chickens before they're hatched

Il ne faut pas vendre la peau de l'ours avant de l'avoir tué
It is not necessary to sell the bearskin without having killed the bear
#

Drive me crazy

Rendre quelqu'un fou
Send someone mad

Drop in the ocean (it's only a..)

Ce n'est qu'une goutte d'eau dans la mer
It's only a drop of water in the sea
#

Drop a large hint

Glisser un mot à l'oreille de quelqu'un
Slip a word in someone's ear
#

Don't wash dirty linen in public

Il faut laver son linge sale en famille
It is necessary to wash dirty linen at home
#

Dutch courage

Bravoure après boire
Bravery after drinking
#

Dying words

Dernières paroles
Last words
#

Do someone a favour

Obliger quelqu'un
Oblige someone

Do-or-die attitude

Attitude de determination inébranlable
Attitude of unwavering determination
#

Don't talk rubbish

Elle bavarde sans cesse
She speaks without stopping
#

Dressed to kill/tarted up

Être sur son trente-et-un
Be on his/her 31
#

Round the bend
Devenir fou
Become mad
#

Don't bite the hand that feeds you

Ne mordez pas la main qui vous nourrit
Don't bite the hand that nourishes you
#

Drunk as a skunk/lord

Ivre mort
Dead drunk

Dressed like a dog's dinner

En grand tralala
All dressed up
#

Discretion is the better part of valour

L'essentiel du courage, c'est la prudence
The essential thing for courage, that's wisdom
#

Dunderhead

Imbécile
Idiot
#

Duty bound (to do it)

Votre devoir vous y oblige
Your duty obliges you to do it

E

Every little helps

Chaque petit geste compte
Every little gesture counts

\#

Early bird catches the worm

L'avenir appartient à ceux qui se lèvent tôt
The future appears to those who rise early

\#

Enough is as good as a feast

Assez vaut un festin
Enough is worthy of a feast

\#

Every Tom, Dick and Harry (go out with)

Frayer avec Pierre, Paul et Jacques
Blaze a trail with Peter, Paul and Jack

\#

Every Tom, Dick and Harry

N'importe qui
No matter who

Everything's going to rack and ruin
Tout va à vau-l'eau
Everything is flowing downstream
#

Screw someone over

Serrer la vis à quelqu'un
Turn the screw on someone
#

Ease off a bit!

Relâche-toi!
Relax a little!
#

Every cloud has a silver lining

Dans toute chose il y a un bon côté
In everything there is a good side
#

Eat someone out of house and home

Manger comme un ogre
Eat like an ogre

F

Face the music

Faire face à quelqu'un/quelque chose
Turn towards someone/something

\#

Fish for information

Chercher à dénicher des renseignements
Look for de-nesting (unearthing) information

\#

Fed up to the back teeth

En avoir marre (de)
Be fed up (with)

\#

First come, first served

Les premiers vont devant
The first ones go in front

\#

Flog a dead horse

Se dépenser en pure perte
Expend effort for pure loss

Fly in the ointment

Un cheveu (sur la soupe)
A hair in the soup
#

From pillar to post

Envoyer quelqu'un de droite à gauche
Send someone from right to left
#

Forgive and forget

Il faut oublier et pardonner
It is necessary to forget and forgive
#

Fit as a fiddle

Être en parfaite santé
Be in perfect health
#

Fly off the handle

Sortir de ses gonds
Fly from the hinges
#

Friends through thick and thin

Copains comme cochons
Friends like pigs

G

Garbage in, garbage out

Entrer ordures, sortir ordures
Put in rubbish, exits rubbish
#

Get on like a house on fire

S'entendre avec quelqu'un
Get along with someone
#

Go down with the 'flu

Attraper la grippe
Catch the 'flu
#

Get my goat (that gets me)

Ça me met en boule
That gets me narked
#

Grin like a Cheshire Cat

Sourire jusqu'aux oreilles
Grin right up to your ears

Get good value for money (here)

En avoir pour son argent
Have enough for your money
#

Get ready for a shock

Attendez-vous à encaisser un choc
Get ready to receive a shock
#

Get on someone's nerves (or wick)

Taper sur les nerfs à quelqu'un
To go on the nerves of someone
#

Go to the dogs

Gâcher sa vie
Ruin his life
#

Get off scot-free

Sans être puni
Without begin punished
#

Get into hot water

Avoir de gros ennuis
Have large annoyances

Give someone a good talking to/dressing down

Flanquer une raclée à quelqu'un
Give a (verbal) hiding to someone
#

God helps those who help themselves

Aide-toi, le ciel t'aidera
Help yourself, the universe will help you
#

Go green with envy

Être dévoré d'envie
To be devoured with envy
#

Go west

Mourir; casser sa pipe
To die; break his pipe
#

Go jump in a lake
Va te faire foutre
Go make yourself scarce

Go hell for leather

Galoper ventre à terre
Gallop stomach to the ground

Get lost

Va te faire foutre
Go make yourself scarce
#

Give someone a piece of your mind

Je lui ai dit ses vérités
I told him some truths
#

Gravy train

L'assiette au beurre
The plate of butter
#

Good-goody two shoes

Faire la sainte nitouche
To do a Saint Nitouche
#

Go the whole hog

Tout risquer
Risk everything

Good-for-nothing

Bon à rien; un vaurien
Good-at-nothing; a rascal

Grin and bear it

Tâcher de garder le sourire
Try to preserve a smile
#

Going great guns

Être en pleine forme
To be in fine form
#

Get something over and done with

C'est une affaire faite
It's a done thing
#

Get your things (and go!)

Envoyer promener quelqu'un
Send someone walking
#

Go see a man about a dog

Aller voir le pape
Go see the pope

H

Handle him with kid gloves

Il faut prendre des gants pour l'approcher
It is necessary to approach him with gloves on

\#

Have butterflies/kittens in your stomach

Avoir l'estomac serré
Have a tight stomach

\#

Have a frog in your throat

Avoir un chat dans la gorge
Have a cat in your throat

\#

Haul someone over the coals

Laver la tête à quelqu'un
Wash someone's head

\#

Hen-pecked husband

Marie mené par sa femme
Husband nagged by his wife

Hell for leather

Galoper ventre à terre
Gallop stomach to the ground
#

Hellava nerve (you have)

Tu as un culot du diable!
You have the Devil's nerve!
#

He wouldn't say boo to a goose

C'est un timide
He's shy
#

He heard a blood-curdling cry

C'était un cri à vous tourner les sangs
It was a cry to turn your bloods
#

He knows which side his bread is buttered on

Il sait où est son avantage
He knows where his advantage lies
#

He threw a sprat to catch a mackerel

Donner un œuf pour avoir un bœuf
Give an egg to catch an ox

He's as happy as a lark/pleased as Punch

Être heureux comme un poisson dans l'eau
Happy as a fish in water
#

He won't budge an inch

Il ne reculerait pas d'un centimètre
He won't withdraw by one centimeter
#

His bark is worse than his bite

Il aboie plus qu'il ne mord
He barks more than he bites
#

He's got a millstone around his neck

C'est un boulet qu'il traînera
It's a cannonball he'll be carrying
#

Have a whale of a time

On s'est drôlement bien amusés
One is really well amused
#

He's a bit snobby/on his high horse

C'est un snobinard
It's a snob

Know-all

Je-sais-tout
I-know-everything
#

He laughs up his sleeve

Il rit dans sa barbe
He laughs into his beard
#

Have the trots

Il a la courante
He has the runs
#

He's a thorn in my side

C'est ma bête noire
It's my black beast
#

Have a bee in your bonnet

Il travaille du chapeau
He works his hat
#

Honour amongst thieves

Les loups ne se mangent pas entre eux
Wolves don't eat each other when together

He has a good head for heights

Il n'a pas le vertige
He doesn't get vertigo
#

Hoot with laughter

Rire aux éclats
Laugh with brilliance
#

He's in deep (water)

Être dans la mélasse
Be in the treacle
#

He's not got all his marbles

Il a une araignée dans le plafond
He's got a spider on the ceiling
#

He's lying; it's all a pack of lies!

C'est un tissu de mensonges!
It's a tissue of lies!
#

He needs a kick up the backside

Flanquer à lui un coup de pied au cul
To give him a kick up the backside

He's on his last legs

Toucher à sa fin
To touch his end
#

He's full of beans

Il est plein de joie
He is full of joy
#

He took to his heels

Prendre ses jambes à son cou
Take your legs to your backside
#

He's completely off his rocker

Con comme la lune
Mad like the moon
#

He's round the bend

Il perd la boule
He's lost his bowling ball
#

He's all fingers and thumbs

Il est maladroit de ses mains
He's clumsy with his hands

Have a bun in the oven

Avoir un polichinelle dans le tiroir
Have a Punch in the drawer
#

Hobson's choice

Un choix qui ne laisse pas d'alternative
A choice that doesn't give an alternative
#

His blood ran cold

Cela se glace le sang
That makes his blood freeze
#

He can't make head nor tail out of it

Il n'y comprend rien
He doesn't understand anything
#

He has a finger in many pies

Il est mêlé à tout
He's mixed in all of it
#

He's his father's son

C'est bien le fils de son père
He is quite the son of his father

He doesn't mince his words

Il ne mâche pas ses mots
He doesn't chew his words
#

He oozes arrogance from every pore

Il est arrogant jusqu'au bout des ongles
He's arrogant to the tip of his nails
#

He's a bit of a dark horse

Il est vraiment énigmatique
He's truly enigmatic
#

He's a sly old dog

C'est un vieux rusé
It's a seasoned dodger
#

He's up to every trick in the book

Il a tout essayé
He's tried everything
#

He shows his true colours

Il se monte sous son vrai jour
Show himself beneath his true day

He's at his wit's end

Il ne sait plus que faire
He doesn't know what to do any more
#

He's been taken for a ride

On l'a eu
One has had him
#

He looked as if butter wouldn't melt in his mouth

On lui donnerait le bon Dieu sans confession
One would give him the holy Father without a confession
#

Higgledy-piggledy

Pêle-mêle
Pell-mell; disorderly
#

He split his sides laughing

Il se tordait de rire
He laughed himself to death

He won't lift a finger/strain himself

Il ne lève jamais le petit doigt
He won't ever lift a little finger

Head over heels in love

Tomber follement amoureux de quelqu'un
Fall madly in love with someone

#

Have a crush on someone

Avoir le béguin pour quelqu'un
Have the bonnet (of a beguine Nun) for someone

#

He'll bend over backwards

Il s'est mis en quatre pour m'aider
He put himself into four to help me

#

He's all sixes and sevens

Il est dans tous ses états
He is in each of his states

#

Have one more (drink) for the road

Un dernier verre pour la ra route
Drink one last glass for the road

#

Hot favourite

Un de ses préferés
One of his favourite things

Hit the jackpot

Gagner le gros lot
Win the big prize
#

Have a heart!

Ayez un peu de cœur !
Have a little heart!
#

Hit or miss

C'est tout ou rien!
It's all or nothing!
#

Hit the roof

Être furieux
Be furious
#

Hit the bottle

Picoler
To tipple/booze

I

I have a bone to pick with you

J'ai maille à partir avec toi
I've stitches to unpick with you
\#

It's raining cats and dogs

Il pleut des cordes
It's raining string
\#

It's nothing ventured, nothing gained

Qui ne risqué rien n'a rien
He who risks nothing gets nothing
\#

It makes me sick to my stomach

J'ai mal au cœur
I'm sick to the heart
\#

It's all just Greek to me

Il pige que dalle
He measures only flagstones

It's the long and short of it

Et voilà tout!
And that's it!
#

I'm sick and tired of you

J'en ai assez de vous
I've had enough of you
#

I wouldn't go there for all the tea in China

Pour rien au monde
For nothing in the world
#

I don't give a damn

Je m'en fous
It's meaningless to me
#

It makes my blood boil

Cela me fait bouillir le sang
That makes my blood boil
#

It went for a song

(Acheter quelque chose) une bouchée de pain
Buy something for a mouthful of bread

I bit off more than I could chew

J'ai les yeux plus gros que je peux mâcher
My eyes are bigger than I can chew

#

In for a penny, in for a pound

Lorsque le vin est tiré, il faut le boire
Once the wine is open, it must be drunk

#

I know it like the back of my hand

Savoir quelque chose par cœur
Know something by heart

#

I'm at the end of my tether

Je suis à bout de forces
I'm at the end of my strength/power

#

It beggars belief

Cela défie toute description
That defies any description

#

In the twinkling of an eye

En un clin d'œil
In the wink of an eye

I told you so! What did I tell you?!

Je vous l'avais bien dit!
I have certainly told it to you
#

It sets my teeth on edge

Cela me fait mal au dents
That makes my teeth hurt
#

I wouldn't touch it with a barge pole

Je ne voudrais pas y toucher avec des pincettes
I wouldn't touch it with a pair of fire tongs
#

If you pay peanuts, you'll get monkeys

Tu les paies une misère
You pay them in misery
#

In the middle of nowhere (a small place)

Un petit trou perdu
A little lost hole
#

I'm flabbergasted

Je suis sidéré
I'm struck down/staggered

It goes without saying that...

Il va de soi que….
It comes from itself that……
#

I will eat my hat

Si ça réussit, je mange le chapeau
If that succeeds, I'll eat my hat
#

In a right pickle/mess/jam

Être dans le pétrin
Be in the kneading trough
#

I haven't got a clue

Je ne sais rien de rien
I know nothing about nothing
#

I'm beside myself with joy/anger

Fou de joie/colère
Mad with joy/anger
#

It's no use crying over spilt milk

À chose faite point de remède
No remedy for things already done

It's all grist to the mill

Ça fait venir l'eau au moulin
That makes water come to the mill
#

It's all gone haywire

Finir en queue de poisson
End up in the fish tail
#

I'm making no headway

Je n'avance pas
I'm not advancing
#

It suits him down to the ground

C'est unique
It's unique
#

I got the shock of my life

J'étais choqué d'apprendre que…
I was shocked to learn that….
#

I can't make head nor tail of it

Je n'y comprends rien
I don't understand any of this

I'm in cracking good form

Je suis en pleine forme
I'm in full form
#

I was caught like a rat in a trap

J'étais pris comme un rat au piège
I was taken like a rat in a trap
#

It's breaking new ground

Faire œuvre de pionnier
Do the work of a pioneer
#

It's a closed book

Être lettre close pour quelqu'un
It's a closed letter for someone
#

It's the pot calling the kettle black

C'est l'hôpital qui se moque de la charité
It's the hospital making fun of charity

J

Jack-of-all-trades

Un bricoleur
A handyman
#

Jam on the brakes

Bloquer les freins
Block the brakes
#

Jammed car (between two lorries)

Voiture coincée entre deux camions
Car cornered between two lorries
#

Jolted into action

Ça m'a donné un coup
That has shaken me up

K

Kill two birds with one stone

Faire d'une pierre deux coups
Make two blows out of one stone
#

Keep up to speed with something

Se tenir au courant de quelque chose
Keep current on something
#

Kiss the dust

Mordre la poussière
Bite the dust
#

Kick the bucket

Casser sa pipe
Break his pipe
#

Kick a man when he's down

Donner le coup de pied de l'âne à quelqu'un
Give a kick to someone's soul

Knit your brows

Froncer les sourcils
Wrinkle your eyebrows
#

Know the ropes

Connaître les ficelles
Know the twine
#

Know something back to front

Être très calé en quelque chose
To be in the know on something
#

Keep your hands off!

N'y touchez pas !
Don't touch that
#

Kick up the backside

Flanquer à quelqu'un un coup de pied au cul
Give someone a kick up the backside

L

Lead someone up the garden path

Monter un bateau à quelqu'un
Pull someone's leg (show a boat to someone)
#

Look before you leap

Il faut réflêchir avant d'agir
It is necessary to reflect before acting
#

Like a bolt from the blue

Un coup de tonnerre
A thunderbolt
#

Like chalk and cheese

C'est le jour et la nuit
Like day and night
#

Like a bat out of hell

À une vitesse vertigineuse
At a dizzying speed

Leave someone in the lurch

Laisser quelqu'un en panne
Leave someone in a breakdown
\#

Like two peas in a pod

Se ressembler comme deux gouttes d'eau
Look like two drops of water
\#

Live in sin

Vivre en concubinage
Live in co-habitation
\#

Live the life of Riley

C'est un vrai luxe!
It's a real luxury!
\#

Live like a Lord

Mener une vie de grand seigneur
Live a life of the grand master/lord
\#

Like clockwork

Tout va comme sur des roulettes
Everything's running on rollers

Like a bull in a china shop

Comme un éléphant dans un magasin de porcelaine
Like an elephant in a china shop
#

Let's play safe

Jouer serré
Play closed
#

Look before you leap

Il faut réfléchir avant d'agir
Think before acting
#

Line your own pockets

Faire sa pelote
Make his own pile
#

Love at first sight

C'est le coup de foudre
It's a thunderbolt
#

Loads of dosh

Un tas d'argent
A heap of money

Like trying to get blood from a stone

On ne saurait tirer de l'huile d'un mur
You can't get oil from a wall
#

Look like a drowned rat

Rentrer trempé comme une soupe
Return dipped in soup
#

Line of least resistance

Choisir la voie de la facilité
Choose the voice of the facility
#

Look daggers at someone

Foudroyer quelqu'un du regard
Strike down someone with a look
#

Laugh your head off

Je suis mort de rire (note: MDR = LOL in English)
I am dead with laughing
#

Like father, like son

Tel père, tel fils
So the father, so the son

M

My heart was in my mouth

J'ai eu un serrement de cœur
I felt a pang in my heart
#

Many hands make light work

À plusieurs mains, l'ouvrage avance
With many hands, the work progresses
#

More hurry, less speed

Plus on se hâte moins on avance
The more one hurries, the less one advances
#

Matter-of-fact

Terre-à-terre
Earth-to-earth
#

Make a mountain out of a molehill

Se faire d'une mouche un éléphant
Make an elephant out of a mosquito

N

Nobody cares

Qu'est-ce que ça fait ?
What does that do?
\#

No news is good news

Point de nouvelles, bonnes nouvelles
Lack of news, good news
\#

Necessity is the mother of invention

Nécessité est mère de l'invention
Necessity is the mother of invention
\#

Never look a gift horse in the mouth

À cheval donné on ne regarde pas à la bride
Don't look at the bridle of a given horse
\#

Next size larger

La pointure au-dessus
The size above

O

On the spur of the moment

Sur le moment
On the moment
#

Once bitten, twice shy

Chat échaudé craint l'eau froide
A scalded cat craves cold water
#

One man's meat is another man's poison

Ce qui guérit l'un tue l'autre
That which heals on kills another
#

Out of the frying pan, into the fire

Tomber de Charybde en Scylla
(Greek mythology) Fall out of Charybdis into Skylla
#

Outstanding debts

Mauvaise créance
Bad debt

P

Paint the town red

Faire la bringue
On the binge
\#

Put someone out of suspense

Tirer quelqu'un de doute
Pull someone from doubt
\#

Pick (or peck) at your food

Pignocher son repas
Pick at a meal
\#

Pots of money

Des tas d'argent
Heaps of money
\#

Proof of the pudding is in the eating

À l'œuvre on connaît l'artisan
One gets to know the artist from the picture

People in glass houses shouldn't throw stones

Il faut être sans défauts pour critiquer autrui
It is necessary to be without faults before criticizing others
#

Pour out his venom

Déverser un torrent d'injures sur quelqu'un
Pour a torrent of insults on someone
#

Put your foot in it

Mettre les pieds dans le plat
Put your feet on the plate
#

Put something to good use

Employer quelque chose à bon usage
Put something to good use
#

Pull the wool over someone's eyes

Jeter de la poudre aux yeux de quelqu'un
Spray powder in someone's eyes
#

Pull out all the stops

Donner le maximum
Give the maximum

Push up the daisies

Il mange les pissenlits par les racines
He's eating dandelions down to the roots

\#

Put the cart before the horse

Mettre la charrue devant les bœufs
Put the plough in front of the oxen

\#

Pull your finger out

Grouille-toi!
Get cracking!

\#

Pull someone to pieces

Critiquer sévèrement quelqu'un
Severely criticize someone

\#

Put that in your pipe and smoke it!

Mettez ça dans votre poche et votre mouchoir par-dessus!
Put that in your pocket and cover it with your handkerchief!

Put the wind up someone

Ficher la frousse à quelqu'un
Put the fear up someone

Put all your eggs in one basket

Mettre tous ses œufs dans le même panier
Put all eggs into one basket
#

Pull someone's leg

Se payer la tête de quelqu'un
Charge the head for someone
#

Put the pedal to the metal/get a move on/put your foot down

Appuyer sur le champignon
Press onto the accelerator
#

Paddle your own canoe

Arriver par soi-même
Arrive by yourself

Q

Queer someone's pitch

Contrecarrer quelqu'un
Thwart someone
#

Quickfire questions

Les questions à une cadence élevée
Questions at a rapid rate
#

Quitter (he's a)

Il est un lâcheur
He's a quitter
#

Quality over quantity

La qualité importe plus que la quantité
Quality is more important than quantity

R

Rise and shine!

Debout les morts!
Stand up you dead!
#

Read the riot act to someone

Semoncer quelqu'un
Lecture someone
#

Run-of-the-mill

C'est ce qu'il y a de plus ordinaire
It's just that something more ordinary
#

Rustle up a good meal

Confectionner un bon repas
Prepare a good meal
#

Rapt in contemplation

Plongé dans la contemplation
Plunged into contemplation

S

Save your own bacon

Sauver sa peau
Save his skin
#

Send a shiver down my spine

Ça m'a fait passer un frisson dans le dos
That has sent a shock down my back
#

Set the ball rolling

Mettre le bal en train
Start the ball moving
#

Sold down the Swanee (or river)

Trahir quelqu'un
Betray someone
#

Screw around

Forniquer
Fornicate

Slink off with your tail between your legs

Il partit l'oreille basse
He left with a low ear

\#

Spitting image of someone

Le portrait vivant de quelqu'un
The living portrait of someone

\#

Sell like hot cakes

Ça se vend comme des petits pains
That's selling like bread rolls

\#

Something the cat brought in

Ça, c'est dégoûtant
That is disgusting

\#

See how the wind blows

Regarder de quel côté vient le vent
See which side the wind approaches

\#

Softie (be a big)

Être sentimental à l'excès
To be excessively sentimental

Saving for a rainy day

Garder une poire pour la soif
Save a pear for your thirst

#

Sh*t bricks

Avoir les jetons
Have the shakes

#

Sink or swim

Il faut risquer le tout pour le tout!
You must risk everything for everything!

#

Shut the stable door after the horse has bolted

Fermer la cage quand les oiseaux se sont envolés
To close the cage after the birds have flown

#

Stone's throw from here

À deux pas d'ici
Two steps from here

#

Son of a bitch

Le fils de pute
Son of a whore

Stand like a stuffed dummy

Planté comme un piquet
Stand like a post

\#

Stand head and shoulders above the rest

Il surpasse tout le monde
He overtakes everyone

\#

Staying in my pit (or bed)

Rester au lit
Stay in bed

\#

Storm in a teacup

Une tempête dans un verre d'eau
Storm in a glass of water

\#

Straight from the horse's mouth

De bonne source
Direct from the source

\#

Shot-gun wedding

Mariage forcé
Wedding of necessity

Stick like a limpet/like glue

Se cramponner (à quelqu'un)
To cling on (to someone)
#

She looked as though butter wouldn't melt in her mouth

On lui donnerait le bon Dieu sans confession
One gave her the Holy Father without confession
#

Shed some light on the matter

Éclairer une affaire
Bring light into a matter
#

Sit on the fence

Ménager la chèvre et le chou
Watch the goat and the cabbage
#

Sow your wild oats

Jeter sa gourme
Cut his teeth

Spick and span

Propre comme un sou neuf
Clean like a new coin
\#

Scared stiff/stupid

Avoir une peur bleue
Have a blue fear
\#

Send someone to Coventry

Mettre quelqu'un en quarantaine
Put someone in isolation
\#

Six of one and half-a-dozen of the other

C'est kif-kif
It's all the same
\#

Sound as a bell

Je suis en parfait santé
I'm in perfect health
\#

Sleep like a log

Dormir à poings fermés
Sleep with closed fists

Sweet talk

La flatterie
Flattery

\#

Something's up

Il y a quelque chose qui ne va pas
There's something not right

\#

Swallow hook, line and sinker

Il a gobé le morceau
He swallowed a piece

\#

Step down a gear

Démultiplier la transmission
Gear down

\#

Stage fright

Il a le trac
He's got the jitters

T

Talk till your blue in the face

Parler jusqu'à devenir bleu
To talk till you become blue

\#

Take someone to the cleaners/fleece someone

Je me suis fait estamper
I've been fleeced

\#

There's neither rhyme nor reason to this

Cela ne rime à rien
That does not rhyme with anything

\#

Thick as thieves

Ils s'entendent comme larrons en foire
They behave like thieves at the fairground

\#

Take someone down a peg or two

Remettre quelqu'un à sa place
Put someone in their place

Taking into account (he was there)

Étant donné qu'il était là
Considering that he was there
#

Three sheets to the wind

Être aux trois quarts ivre
Be three quarters drunk
#

Till the cows come home

Attendre jusqu'à la semaine des quatre jeudis
Wait until the week with four Thursdays
#

That was a close shave

Il était moins cinq!
That was minus five!
#

That's the snag/the crux of the matter

Le nœud de la question
The knot of the question

There's one born every minute

Quel idiot/quelle idiote!
What an idiot
#

Tell me another!

À d'autres!
To other things
#

Tax someone's patience (to the limit)

Pousser à bout la patience de quelqu'un
Push someone's patience to the extreme
#

Too many cooks spoil the broth

Trop de cuisinières gâtent la sauce
Too many cooks spoil the sauce
#

To have at your fingertips/go like clockwork

Tout marche comme sur des roulettes
Everything's running on rollers
#

There wasn't a soul on the street

Il n'y avait pas un chat dans la rue
There wasn't a cat in the street

That's a fine mess

Être dans le pétrin
Be in the dough
#

That's a right kettle of fish

Nous voilà dans de beaux draps!
To be in a fine mess
#

Two's company, three's a crowd

Deux s'amusent , trois s'embêtent
Two amuse each other; three annoy each other
#

The real McCoy

Le vrai de vrai
The truth of truth
#

That put a spoke in his wheel

Mettre des bâtons dans les roues
Put sticks in the wheels
#

Throw a spanner in the works

Mettre des bâtons dans les roues
Put sticks in the wheels

Throw in the sponge (or towel)

S'avouer vaincu
Acknowledge defeat
#

There are no flies on him

Il n'est pas bête
He's not an animal
#

That's half baked

Insuffisamment étudié
Insufficiently studied
#

This is no picnic

Cela n'a guère été une partie de plaisir
That has hardly been pleasurable
#

Throw someone off the scent

Perdre la trace de quelqu'un
Lose trace of someone
#

Thingummajig

Le truc
The thing

That looks like something the cat brought in

Ça, c'est dégoûtant
That's disgusting
#

That's far fetched

Ça, c'est tiré par les cheveux
That's swung by the hair
#

To get out of the wrong side of the bed

Il s'est levé du pied gauche
He got up with his left foot
#

This happens once in a blue moon

Tous les trente-six du mois
This happens once every thirty-six months
#

The ball's in your court now

C'est à toi/vous de jouer
Now it's your turn to play
#

The coast is clear

Le champ est libre
The field is free

That's the last straw to break the camel's back

Une goutte d'eau suffit pour faire déborder le vase
One drop of water suffices to make the vase overflow
#

That's just about the limit

Ça c'est le combie!
That is the limit
#

Talk for England/talk your head off

Bavarder sans cesse
Talk without stopping
#

That takes the biscuit

Ça, c'est le bouquet!
Now that's the crowning piece
#

Turn me down flat

Il m'a refusé catégoriquement
He categorically refused me
#

Today of all days
Il fallait que ça tombe aujourd'hui
It had to happen today

That's a bit odd/fishy

C'est curieux/bizarre
That is odd
#
This place gives me the creeps

Donner la chair de poule à quelqu'un
Make someone's flesh creep
#
That's wickedly expensive

C'est hors de prix
That's outside of price
#
Tread on someone's toes

Marcher sur les pieds de quelqu'un
Step on someone's feet
#
Turn a blind eye

Fermer les yeux (sur)
Close your eyes (on something)

U

Ugly as hell/sin

Celle est laide comme les sept péchés capitaux
She's as ugly as the seven deadly sins

#

Under Virgo (born under)

Les gens du signe de la Vierge
People of the sign of the virgin

#

Under the Doctor's orders

Sous les ordres du médcin
Under the doctor's orders

#

Under an assumed name

Sous un pseudonyme
Under a false name

V

Vanish into thin air

Se volatiliser
Fade away
#

Value judgement

Judgement de valeur
Judgement of value
#

Vain (take God's name in vain)

Prendre le nom de Dieu en vain
Take the name of God in vain
#

Vogue expression

Mot à la mode
Fashionable word/statement

W

Wallflower (be a)

Faire tapisserie
Make like the wallpaper
\#

What got into him?

Quelle mouche l'a piqué?
Which mosquito bit him?
\#

While the cat's away the mice will play

Quand le chat n'est pas là, les souris dansent
When the cat's not there the mice dance
\#

Wear your heart on your sleeve

Laisser voir ses sentiments
Allow sentiment to be seen
\#

Wet behind the ears

Si on lui pressait le nez, il en sortirait encore du lait
If you pressed his nose, more milk would come out

Whole nine yards/baggage

Le principe des neuf verges
The principle of the nine yards
#

WYSIWYG (what you see if what you get)

Tel écran, tel écrit
This screen, this writing
#

Without further ado (or ceremony)

Sans plus de façons/d'embarras
Without further embarrassment
#

Win hands down

Gagner haut la main
Win hands high
#

Walk the plank

Passer à la planche
Pass on the plank
#

With a single stroke of the pen

Un trait de plume
With a single feather stroke

X

X marks the spot

L'endroit est marqué d'une croix
The spot is marked with a cross

\#

X-ray (take an X-ray of something)

Passer à la radio
To X-ray something

\#

X-rated film

Film interdit aux moins de 18 ans
Film forbidden under 18 years old

\#

XXXX

Grosses bises
Large kisses

\#

X number of people

Pour x personnes
For x people

Y

You can bet your life on that

J'en donnerais ma tête à couper que…
I would give my head to count that…..
#

You can't make a silk purse out of a sow's ear

On ne saurait faire d'une buse un épervier
You can't make a sparrowhawk from a buzzard
#

You can say goodbye to all that
Dire adieu à quelque chose
Say goodbye to something

You could have knocked me down with a feather

J'ai pensé tomber de mon haut
I thought I would fall from my height
#

You need locking up/belong in the mad house

Être dans la maison de fous
Be in the house of fools

You can't have your cake and eat it

On ne peut pas avoir le drap et l'argent
One cannot have the cloth (brocade) and the money
\#

You can't teach an old dog new tricks

Il est difficile de déranger les vieilles habitudes
It's difficult to change old habits
\#

You can't make a silk purse out of a sow's ear

On ne saurait faire d'une buse un épervier
One can never make a sparrowhawk from a buzzard
\#

Younger son/daughter

Fils cadet/fille cadette
Younger son/daughter
\#

Yum-yum

Miam-miam!
Delicious!

Z

Zero in on something

Régler le tir sur quelque chose
Hone the shot on something
#

Zero hour

L'heure H
The H hour
#

Zoom through something

Passer en trombe
Go by in a whirlwind
#

Zoom along (cars)

Les voitures passent en trombe sur la route
Cars pass in a whirlwind along the road

ABOUT THE AUTHOR

Jackie studied French and German in secondary school and went on to gain a Bachelor of Arts Honours Degree from the prestigious University of Exeter. She completed an additional year at St. Luke's College to gain her Post Graduate Certificate in Education, specialising in Modern Languages, majoring in German and French.

After completing teacher training she joined the Royal Air Force as a language specialist. Her favourite memories of all things French stem from the Bristol-Bordeaux schools' Exchange, when she stayed with the Martineau family on many occasions, learning how French people really speak! She is still in touch with that family today. Jackie was also selected to interpret for NATO and completed her Civil Service Commission German Interpreter's exam in military terminology.

After leaving the Air Force, Jackie went on to establish a successful business career implementing learning development strategies mainly in the motor industry. She is currently the Curriculum Manager at the Henry Ford Academy, working for Ford Motor Company, based in Daventry, UK.

Jackie has written two other books - **The Little Black Rammbook** and **Raining Cats and Dogs (German)** available on Amazon. Visit her website www.rammbook.yolasite.com where the French and German versions of 'Raining Cats and Dogs' will feature. She would love to speak to anyone fluent in another language to work together on more 'Raining Cats and Dogs' books! Contact Jackie via her website, or through Linked In.

Printed in Great Britain
by Amazon